MODERN RUSSIAN MASTERWORKS

ARAM KHATCHATURIAN

SONATINA (1959)
FOR PIANO

Edited by György Sandor

ISBN 978-0-7935-5008-1

G. SCHIRMER, Inc.

DISTRIBUTED BY

HAL•LEONARD®
CORPORATION
7777 W. BLUEMOUND RD. P.O. BOX 13819 MILWAUKEE, WI 53213

Sonatina
for Piano

Aram Khatchaturian (1959)
Edited by György Sandor

1

47588cx

4

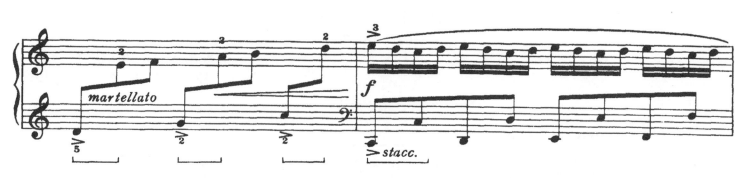

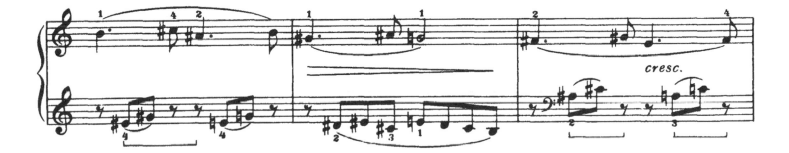

a tempo   **poco animato**   **a tempo**

secco   *marcato*   *f*

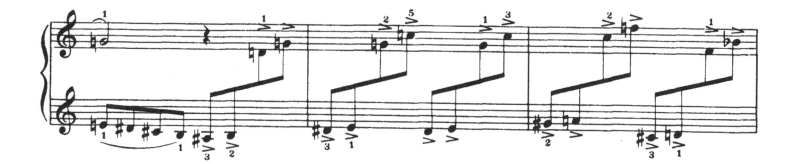

f

stacc. quasi pizz.

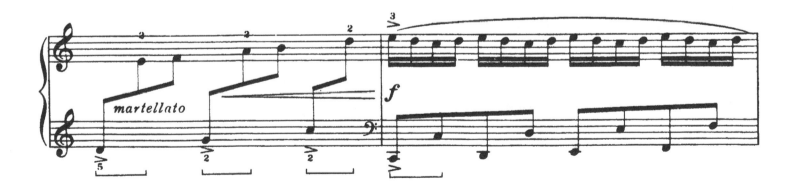

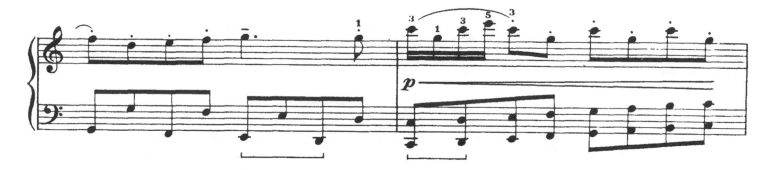

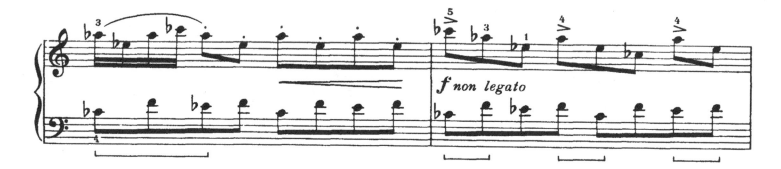

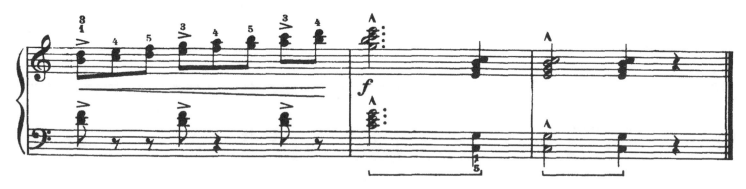

2

Andante con anima, rubato ♩ = 108

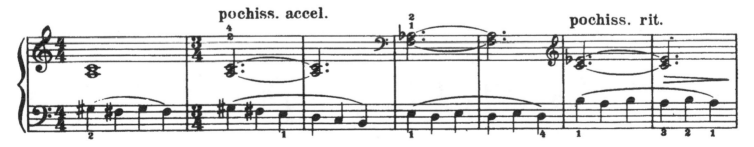

3

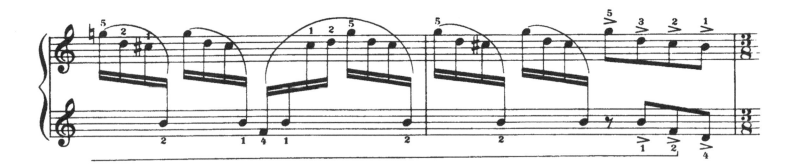

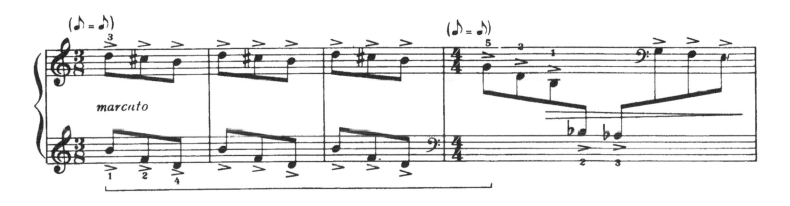

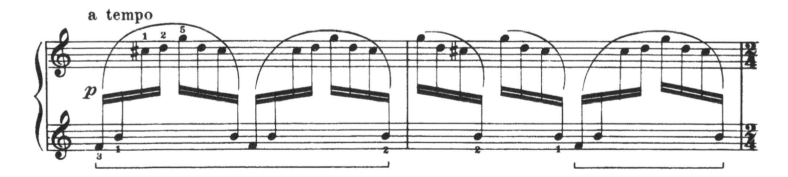

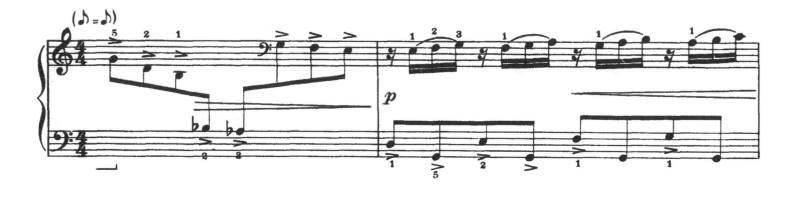

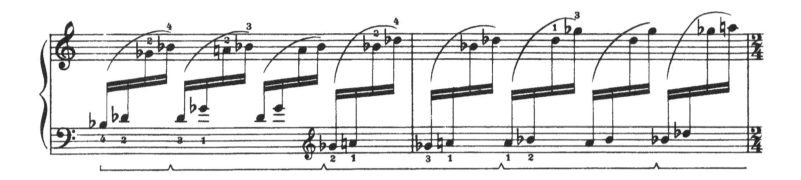

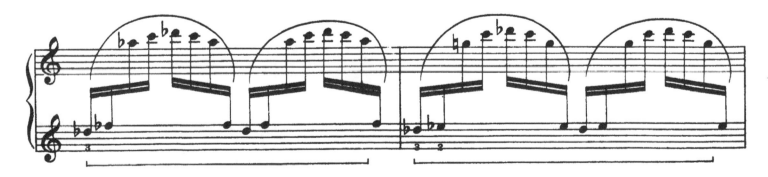

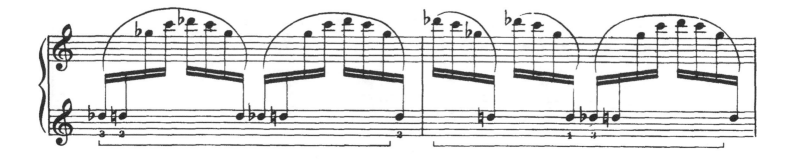

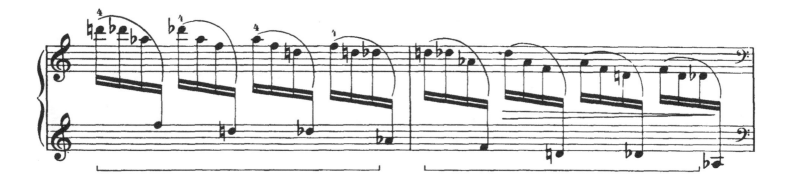

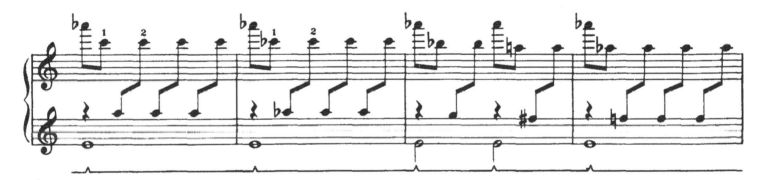

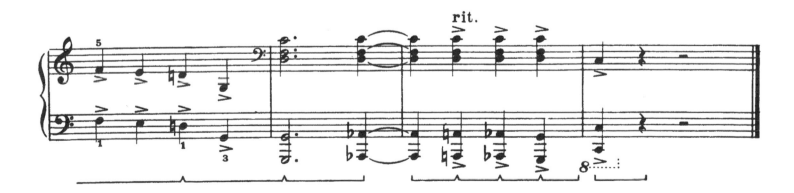